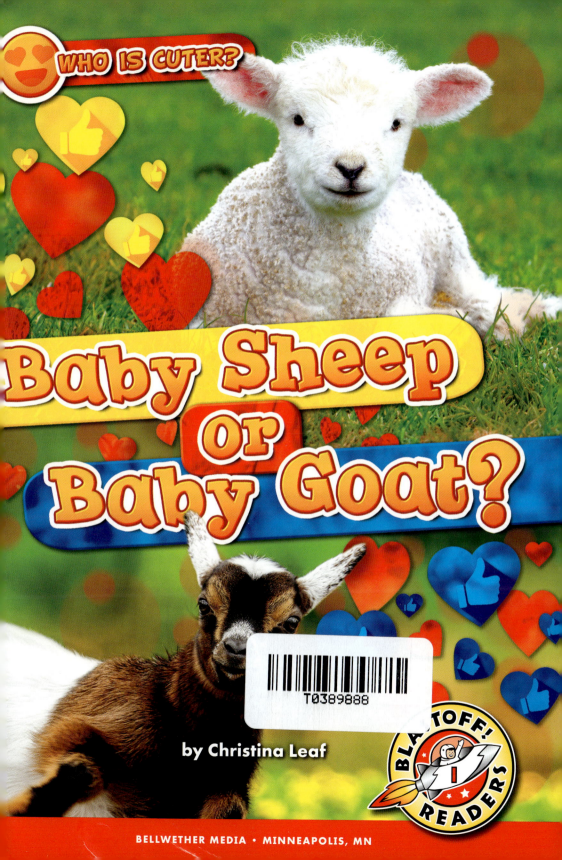

Blastoff! Readers are carefully developed by literacy experts to build reading stamina and move students toward fluency by combining standards-based content with developmentally appropriate text.

 Level 1 provides the most support through repetition of high-frequency words, light text, predictable sentence patterns, and strong visual support.

 Level 2 offers early readers a bit more challenge through varied sentences, increased text load, and text-supportive special features.

 Level 3 advances early-fluent readers toward fluency through increased text load, less reliance on photos, advancing concepts, longer sentences, and more complex special features.

★ **Blastoff! Universe**

This edition first published in 2025 by Bellwether Media, Inc.

No part of this publication may be reproduced in whole or in part without written permission of the publisher. For information regarding permission, write to Bellwether Media, Inc., Attention: Permissions Department, 6012 Blue Circle Drive, Minnetonka, MN 55343.

Library of Congress Cataloging-in-Publication Data

Names: Leaf, Christina, author.
Title: Baby sheep or baby goat? / Christina Leaf.
Description: Minneapolis, MN : Bellwether Media, Inc., 2025. | Series: Blastoff! readers: who is cuter? | Includes bibliographical references and index. | Audience: Ages 5-8 | Audience: Grades K-1 | Summary: "Developed by literacy experts for students in kindergarten through grade three, this book introduces the differences between baby sheep and baby goats to young readers through leveled text and related photos"– Provided by publisher.
Identifiers: LCCN 2024003095 (print) | LCCN 2024003096 (ebook) | ISBN 9798886870336 (library binding) | ISBN 9798893041477 (paperback) | ISBN 9781644878774 (ebook)
Subjects: LCSH: Lambs–Juvenile literature. | Kids (Goats)–Juvenile literature.
Classification: LCC SF376.5 .L433 2025 (print) | LCC SF376.5 (ebook) | DDC 636.3/07-dc23/eng/20240304
LC record available at https://lccn.loc.gov/2024003095
LC ebook record available at https://lccn.loc.gov/2024003096

Text copyright © 2025 by Bellwether Media, Inc. BLASTOFF! READERS and associated logos are trademarks and/or registered trademarks of Bellwether Media, Inc. Bellwether Media is a division of Chrysalis Education Group.

Editor: Suzane Nguyen   Designer: Andrea Schneider

Printed in the United States of America, North Mankato, MN.

Table of Contents

Lambs and Kids! 4
Wool and Horns 8
Grasses and Leaves 14
Who Is Cuter? 20
Glossary 22
To Learn More 23
Index 24

Lambs and Kids!

Sheep and goats have cute babies! Baby sheep are called lambs. Baby goats are kids!

kids

lambs

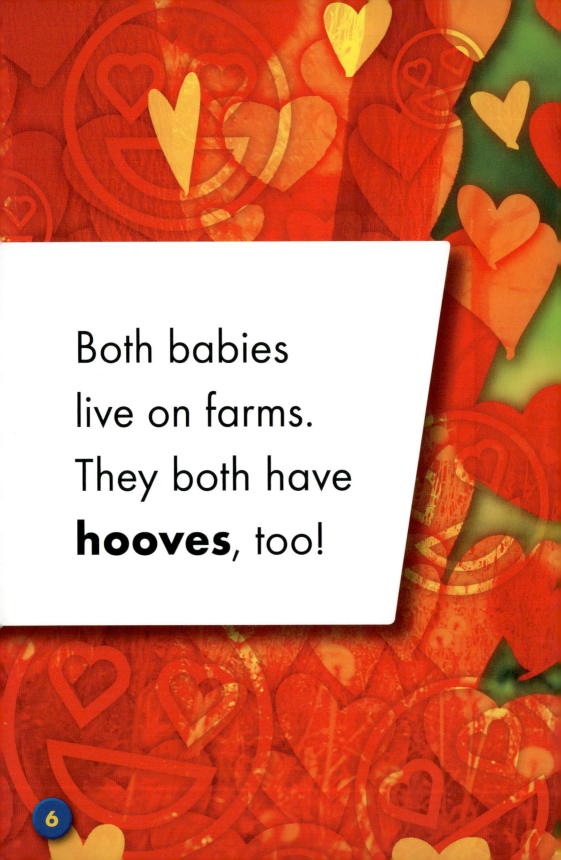

Both babies live on farms. They both have **hooves**, too!

hooves

Wool and Horns

Most lambs are covered in curly **wool**. Kids have **straight** hair.

Lamb tails hang down.
Kid tails stand up!

Most lambs do not grow **horns**. Most kids grow horns!

Grasses and Leaves

Lambs **graze**.
They eat grasses.
Kids may graze.
But they would rather eat leaves.

eating leaves

grazing

Older lambs are **sheared**. Their wool gets hot! Most kids do not need to be sheared.

Lambs say baa.
Kids say meh.
Which cutie
do you like?

Who Is Cuter?

does not grow horns

curly wool

baa

tail hangs down

Baby Sheep

grazes on grasses

gets sheared

Glossary

graze
to feed on grasses

sheared
to have wool cut off

hooves
hard coverings on the feet of some animals

straight
without bends or curls

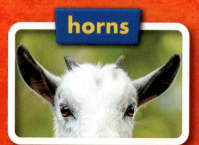
horns
hard, bony body parts on the heads of some animals

wool
soft, curly hair or fur

To Learn More

AT THE LIBRARY

Barnes, Rachael. *Baby Goats*. Minneapolis, Minn.: Bellwether Media, 2023.

Hicks, Kelli. *Born On a Farm*. New York, N.Y.: Crabtree Publishing, 2023.

Rathburn, Betsy. *Baby Sheep*. Minneapolis, Minn.: Bellwether Media, 2024.

ON THE WEB

FACTSURFER

Factsurfer.com gives you a safe, fun way to find more information.

1. Go to www.factsurfer.com.

2. Enter "baby sheep or baby goat" into the search box and click 🔍.

3. Select your book cover to see a list of related content.

Index

baa, 18, 19
farms, 6
goats, 4
grasses, 14
graze, 14, 15
hair, 8, 9
hooves, 6, 7
horns, 12, 13
leaves, 14, 15
meh, 18, 19
sheared, 16
sheep, 4
tails, 10
wool, 8, 9, 16

The images in this book are reproduced through the courtesy of: Pozdeyev Vitaly, front cover (lamb), p. 11; Rita_Kochmarjova, Rita Kochmarjova/ Adobe Stock, front cover (kid); pp. 5, 6-7, 10-11, 22 (horns); Eric Isselee, pp. 3 (lamb), 20 (gets sheared), 21 (kid); ynke van Holten, p. 3 (kid); agcreations, pp. 4-5, 13; a4ndreas, p. 7; Milan Noga reco/ Adobe Stock, pp. 8-9; kwadrat70/ Adobe Stock, p. 9; Jason Lovell/ Adobe Stock, pp. 12-13; Ben Schonewille | Dreamstime.com, pp. 14-15; s-cphoto, p. 15; Klein & Hubert/ Nature Picture Library, pp. 16-17; BushAlex, p. 17; nmelnychuk/ Adobe Stock, pp. 18-19; pelooyen, p. 19; Erik Lam, p. 20 (lamb); Melinda Nagy, p. 20 (grazes on grasses); Ilse_Innire, p. 21 (eats leaves); Maksym/ Adobe Stock, p. 21 (does not need to be sheared); Juha Remes | Dreamstime.com, p. 22 (graze); Wirestock | Dreamstime.com, p. 22 (hooves); Sevaljevic, p. 22 (sheared); Goldilock Project, p. 22 (straight); Anne Coatesy/ Adobe Stock, p. 22 (wool).

24